BIS Publishers

LIE LIKE AN ARTIST

Rod Judkins

WHAT DO YOU WANT TO SAY?
Define your core message

WHO? Find a way to find yourself

TO WHOM? Find the right audience for your message

IN WHAT MEDIUM? Find the best medium to give your message impact

WITH WHAT EFFECT? Have the effect you intended.

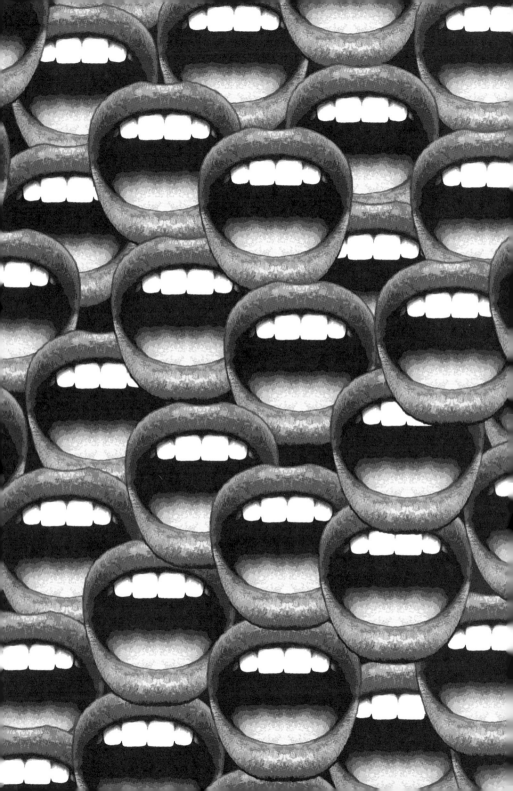

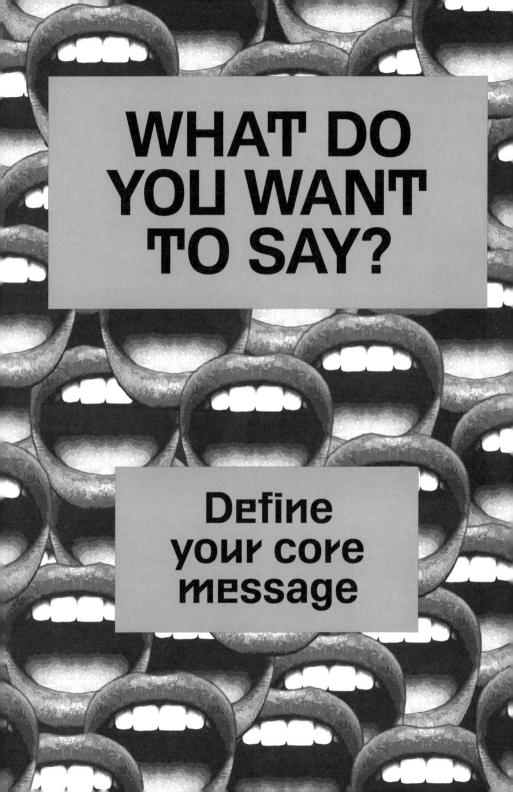

WHAT DO YOU WANT TO SAY?

Define your core message

To communicate the truth,

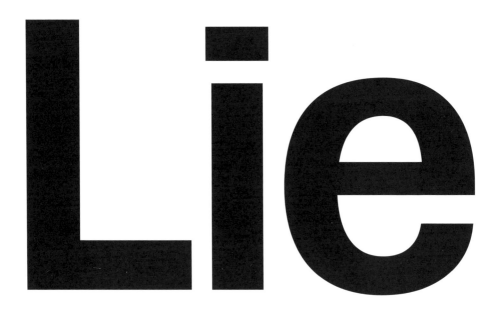

"We all know that art is not truth. Art is a lie that makes us realize truth." said Pablo Picasso. I love this sentence because it reminds me of the purpose of creativity, whether art, fiction, design, film, or advertising. Different versions of this maxim have been attributed to creative people in almost every field, from Jean Cocteau to Albert Camus.

If you paint a portrait of someone, it's a canvas covered with paint. It's not the actual person; it's an illusion (the lie). But the painting can reveal more (the truths) about that person than if you met them. The artist's role is to help us see these hidden truths.

A novel is a lie. Adverts, operas, films, TV – all lies. But these artist's intentions are the most worthwhile possible – to reveal truths. Artists understand that profound truths are communicated better with creativity. This book explains how artists express their ideas persuasively. It describes the techniques they use to convey truths better, make sure they are noticed, have an impact, and fix those ideas in the minds of an audience.

Our lives would be improved if we lied like artists because they focus on discovering truths and working out how to communicate them so they're etched on our minds.

PUT YOUR TRUTH HERE

"The deeper the truth in a creative work, the longer it will live."
Charlie Chaplin

The public misunderstands art. It's considered superfluous and self-indulgent. It's the exact opposite. Creatives dig for the meaning and substance in our lives – the deeper truths. Then they communicate them so they are unforgettable. The techniques to achieve this are in Lie Like an Artist.

I'm often asked, "How can I get ideas and be motivated?" My answer is straightforward. Set out to better understand yourself or the world around you. Then, share these truths. It's simple. Look at the world with this attitude – ideas and inspiration are everywhere.

Get ideas

Significant truths are difficult to convey. So, creative people develop ways to communicate these truths. They are lies (illusions) but with the best possible intention – to give you a deeper insight than the facts.

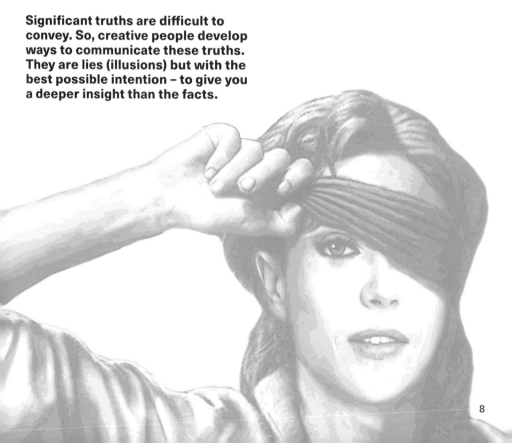

and

Many people lie to hide the truth, to pull a blindfold over your eyes. The creative person's goal is to lift the blindfold and reveal truths either about our inner world of thoughts and emotions or the outer world.

be

motivated

The reason artists are so motivated is because of the sense of purpose revealing truths gives them. "The aim of art is to represent not the outward appearance of things, but their inward significance." said Aristotle. We look at films, paintings, novels, and TV programs because the artist has given us a deeper awareness of what it is to be human. They reveal to us who we are. That's what motivates creative people and it's the reason they work day and night with passion.

I don't know about you, but I often feel a desperate urge to be creative, but I can't think of a subject matter. Whenever this happens, I turn to John Baldessari. He clarifies things for me.

Baldessari pointed out that an artist points things out.
He produced a series of paintings of a hand pointing at objects such as a cooker, a light bulb, a crack in a wall, and other things.

wh

the

"What an artist is trying to do for people is bring them closer to something, because of course art is about sharing: you wouldn't be an artist if you didn't want to share an experience, a thought." David Hockney

An artist draws attention to something they find interesting. I love this idea of creativity because it's down to earth. Photos posted online, an oil painting in the national gallery, a fridge magnet, a sculpture in the street – they're a finger pointing at something the artist is enthusiastic about and want to share.

at's oint?

If you're stuck, remember, all you have to do is point. Your audience will feel closer to you and your work if you show what you love. I'm a fan of John Baldessari, so I'm sharing my enthusiasm with you.

A combination of upbringing and character means I smile and nod instead of demanding what I want. I have goals I don't go for because I feel pressured into being dutiful. It becomes a habit to accept less than we want. We feel embarrassed by our ambitions. We're afraid to state what we want because family, friends, or colleagues make us think it's ridiculous or we're being unrealistic.

Why you don't get what you want

A young, unknown singer appeared on a TV show to promote her overlooked debut album, released six months previously. Her record label had so little confidence in her they didn't invest money in a promo video.

The wannabe pop star was asked about her ambitions and replied, "To rule the world…" She sounded ridiculous and unrealistic. The music industry was patronising and laughed. But she wasn't afraid to state what she wanted. Her truthfulness set her apart.

The singer was Madonna. She became the all-time bestselling female artist, the most successful solo artist in US chart history, and the highest-grossing solo performing artist. She explained her success, "A lot of people are afraid to say what they want. That's why they don't get what they want."

Later, Madonna explained, "…I just meant I want to make a mark on the world, I want to be a somebody. Because I grew up feeling like a nobody, and I wanted to make a difference."

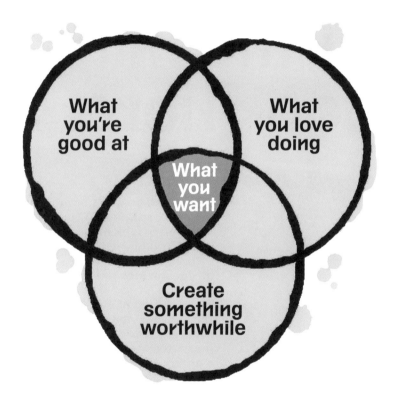

It can be challenging, but it's cathartic to say what you want out loud. Your desires define you. Suppress them, and you're not you.

If you don't pursue your goals, you'll spend your time fulfilling other people's.

I stare at ceilings for hours. I spend my holidays in Venice. In the 17th century, artists were ordered to make their audience look up to what was important. So, the ceilings in palaces and churches show religious figures, mythological gods, emperors, and kings. They're distant and ethereal. I love those paintings – Veronese is my all-time favourite painter. But there's something I love more.

Searching for meaning? Look here...

In the 20th century, artists chose their own subjects. They looked low. They felt to look high was to look away. Psychiatrist Carl Jung said, "Modern man can't see God because he doesn't look low enough."

The meaning of our lives is not in the heavens. Significance is in the everyday world surrounding us. A can of soup, a balloon dog, or a urinal. Art is not an escape into fantasy; it's an escape into reality.

"I can get excitement watching rain on a puddle. And then I paint it. Now, I admit, there are not too many people who would find that exciting. But I would. And I want life thrilling and rich. And it is. I make sure it is." David Hockney

I was astounded by Joana Vasconcelos's work when I saw her exhibition at the Guggenheim in Bilbao. Her sculpture, Marilyn, was a massive pair of elegant, high-heeled shoes made from saucepans – a symbol of female domesticity. A Marilyn Monroe stiletto is a sign of female glamour. Vasconcelos mashed them together. She makes us look deeply at everyday objects because they reveal the meaning and essence of our lives.

Are you looking low enough?

I've noticed something about successful artist's careers. Like everyone, they struggle to get off the ground for a while. But suddenly, they take off like a rocket. I realised they use a special launchpad.

Make your message unforgettable

The transformation of Van Gogh's work has always been a great example. The colours in his early paintings were dark, sludgy browns. His work rocketed up a few levels when he realised he should find something distinctive about his subject, then exaggerate it.

He intensified his colours. Yellow sunflowers became yellower. Swirling clouds became a violent vortex. A night became sky darker, and the stars brighter. Van Gogh exaggerated truths, and that made us more aware of them. Boosting the truth boosted his work.

"I want to paint it so big that people will have no choice but to stop and look and really see it – as it is." Georgia O'Keefe on painting a flower.

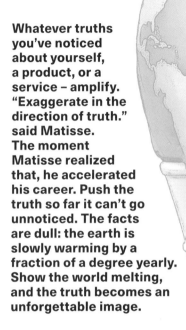

Whatever truths you've noticed about yourself, a product, or a service – amplify. "Exaggerate in the direction of truth." said Matisse. The moment Matisse realized that, he accelerated his career. Push the truth so far it can't go unnoticed. The facts are dull: the earth is slowly warming by a fraction of a degree yearly. Show the world melting, and the truth becomes an unforgettable image.

Walking around a gallery, I'm in a world where the truth has been exaggerated. A bronze spider 20 feet tall – represents Louise Bourgeois's mother. Abstraction pushed as far as it will go by de Kooning. A human figure reduced to basic geometric shapes by Braque.

THERE IS NO "CORRECTLY"

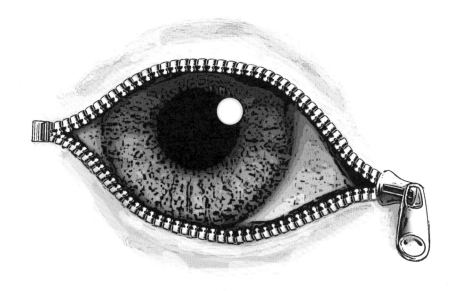

**Your doctor explains you are
going blind. How do you react?**

In later life, Monet was horrified when doctors told him
cataracts in both his eyes would lead to blindness. But he soon
embraced his situation and became fascinated. He wrote,
"My poor eyesight makes me see everything in a complete fog.
It's very beautiful all the same..." Monet was inspired by his
new, blurred vision. It led to radical insights.

Whenever I'm in New York, I visit Monet's three giant paintings, "Water Lilies 1914–26", at the Guggenheim. Over a hundred years later, they still look radical. There are no hard edges, and everything appears to be dissolving. But most radical of all is his thinking.

Monet was not the first artist to have cataracts. The others stopped painting because they couldn't see correctly. To Monet, there was no "correctly." He painted what he saw truthfully. What he saw was a blur. So, he painted a blur.

Monet challenged traditional art's static view of the world during his career. His paintings showed how everything constantly changed, and nothing was fixed. Look at a building, and the light changes from minute to minute. Revisit the scene, and you will notice different details and themes.

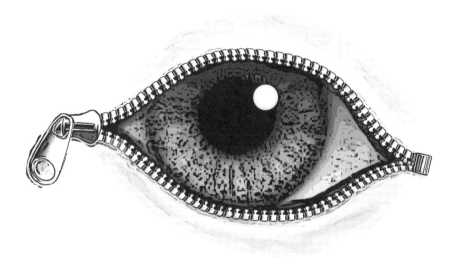

There is always something new to observe. "No man ever steps in the same river twice, for it's not the same river, and he's not the same man." said Heraclitus. Monet's love of change gave him an agile mind. He had the right mindset to embrace a life-changing transformation like blindness.

Our attitude affects how we see.

When I first wrote this chapter, it was five pages long. It's taken days to reduce it. I've slashed out passages I loved – but weren't to the point. To cut through, I knew it had to be razor-sharp.

Sharpen your idea so it cuts through

It takes hard work to write clearly. I've taught in universities for years. It's an academic tradition to write complex sentences seeped in jargon. "An intellectual says a simple thing in a hard way. An artist says a hard thing in a simple way." said Charles Bukowski. An academic attitude is – if the audience can't understand, it's because they're not clever enough. Not true. The writer needs to be more clever if the audience can't understand. If one of my students writes an introduction to an essay that's unnecessarily long, I suggest they rewrite it using emojis.

When Jenny Holzer was a student at university, she was given a "wonderful yet daunting" reading list. She "reacted against it" and summed up the essence of each book in one line. Then, she displayed the list on posters spread across New York. Holzer's work was called Truisms (1977–87). Here are a few... "Abuse of Power Should Come as No Surprise," "Romantic love was invented to manipulate women", "A strong sense of duty imprisons you," and "Protect me from what I want." The truths are startling. Truisms caused a sensation and rocketed Holzer to international attention.

The thinking behind advertising slogans is similar – sum up the truth of a product in a concise phrase that triggers feelings and connects with an audience. Writing a strapline is more demanding than writing a novel. I'm a big fan of Salmon Rushdie's books. The best thing he ever wrote was the line, "That'll do nicely" for American Express. It's friendly without being smug. Getting your idea across in three words is more challenging than using twenty thousand. They have more impact.

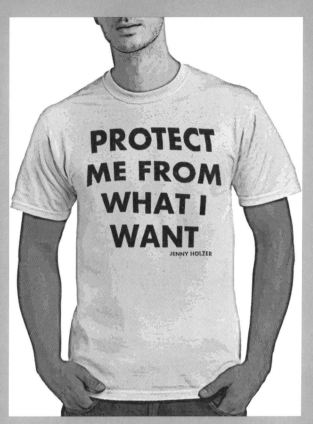

PROTECT
ME FROM
WHAT I
WANT
JENNY HOLZER

Other succinct lines... "Because You're Worth It" L'Oreal's truths – an empowering message of self-confidence and self-worth. "Let's Go Places." Toyota's truth is that the benefit of an inexpensive, reliable car is that you can confidently drive anywhere. "Belong Anywhere." AirBnB's truths: Stay in someone's home instead of a tourist hotel, and your visit will be authentic.

An idea needs to be sharpened. Deciding what to say means deciding what not to say. Be merciless. "Art is the exclusion of the unnecessary." said Carl Andre. Include less, and you'll convey more with impact.

When I first learned to cycle, I concentrated. I was hyper-conscious of where I was going, directing the handlebars, pedestrians crossing the road, the pedals, passing cars – everything. My conscious mind transferred that knowledge to my mechanical mind. When I'm cycling now, I'm like a robot. I arrive at my destination and can't remember anything about the journey. If I'm not careful, I become as machine-like as the cycle. I often walk into my studio and don't see it. I know it too well. Familiarity and habit make me see and act mechanically, like a robot.

You're turning into a robot

"I live in the same state of innocence as the child who believes he can reach out from his cot and grasp a bird in the sky." René Magritte

There are no good habits. All habits are bad because they make us mechanical. To be creative, we must be hyper-aware. "The effort to see things without distortion takes something like courage, and this courage is essential to the artist, who has to look at everything as though he saw it for the first time." said Henri Matisse.

Seeing is active; it's more than opening your eyes. Sight isn't enough. We need insight. Matisse often repeatedly painted the same scene, person, or object but with different results each time. He never repeated himself because he looked at his subject every second of every day as if he'd never seen it before. Whenever I see a Matisse, my eyes light up.

PAST
Regret
Dwelling on mistakes
Replaying events
Over-analysing

PRESENT
See clearly
Perceptive
Aware

FUTURE
Worry about what might happen
Anxious about "what if" situations

RESIST!

We never see anything twice because everything changes. But habit is about sticking to what you know and repeating the past. The past is a burden of accumulated experiences that interfere with our perception. Art is about being so embedded in the present that we are freed from the past. Artists persistently destroy their own traditions because tradition is a mindless habit.

The purpose of creativity is not to fill the world with art. It's to prevent us from seeing mechanically.

Sometimes, I might walk through Slough and think, "This place is boring." But it's not Slough that's boring. The sense of boredom is in me. Dismissing things because they're not engaging is a slippery slope, leading to dismissing almost everything.

Get ideas, anywhere, anytime

"If you stare at an object, as you do when you paint, there is no point at which you stop learning things from it." Wayne Thiebaud

Have you ever looked closely at a beetle? The design company NBD Nano learned about the humble Namib desert beetle. It survives in the African desert by condensing water on its back, harvesting it, and storing it. NBD Nano was inspired and mimicked the technique to design a self-filling water bottle capable of creating up to three litres every hour.
A humble little insect but a gigantic inspiration.

Inspiration doesn't happen; you have to make it happen. Set out to learn from the things around you, and inspiration follows. Stimulation does not come from outside you but from inside you. It's not what you look at but how you look.

24

The uninspired...

Get through the day.
Enjoy buying things.
Want to be entertained.
Are satisfied with themselves.
Despair about what's wrong.
Are busy.
Find reasons to delay.
Do whatever is easiest.

The inspired...

Get something out of the day.
Enjoy making things.
Want to entertain.
Want to develop themselves.
Improve what's wrong.
Are productive.
Find reasons to act.
Enjoy confronting challenges.

We are surrounded by inspiring things we don't notice.
The answers to our problems are all around us – under
our noses, but we're not paying attention.

Clear

CAUTION
DUE TO SEVERE
BRAIN FOG
ALL MY THOUGHTS
ARE SUSPENDED
INDEFINITELY

your

The artists that impress me most have a purpose: to clear the fog – in their minds and ours. They revealed something unique to me that had been shrouded in mist.

Oscar Wilde looked at the fog and didn't see it. Whistler produced paintings of London in fog in the late 1800s. After seeing Whistler's fog paintings, Wilde became aware of its mystery, beauty, and enigma. "There may have been fogs for centuries in London... But no one saw them, and so we know nothing about them. They did not exist until art had invented them." said Oscar Wilde.

Londoners had not appreciated the fog surrounding them. "...People see fogs, not because there are fogs, but because poets and painters have taught them the mysterious loveliness of such effects." said Oscar Wilde. People only saw fog as a nuisance until Whistler showed everyone its qualities. Today, fog or mist is regularly used in films to add mystery and intrigue.

Our minds suffer from brain fog. We need to be aware of the wonders in the everyday world that are overlooked (like fog). There are many things "in the way." Instead of seeing them as "in the way," make them "the way."

A quiet voice

iи a

When I start a project like this book, I sometimes think it's got to be loud to be noticed in a bookshop. It's the wrong attitude. It messes up my thinking. I remind myself of a minor, humble jacket that had a massive impact on me. It showed me a message doesn't have to shout to be loud. A voice can be quiet because the message has an effect.

At age fifty, Agnes Richter was earning a living as a seamstress. In 1893, her family had her incarcerated at Heidelberg psychiatric hospital. The hospital took away her clothes and made her wear a hospital gown. Our clothes express our personality, so it was the institution's way of removing her identity.

She cut up her gown and tailored it into a beautifully fitting garment. Then, she stitched defiant statements in delicate lines across the rough surface. The subverted gown was a way of holding on to her identity. Richter channelled her frustration into the only outlet she had. The audience for her statements was the staff and patients.

It is now an exhibit in the Prinzhorn Collection in Heidelberg. But it has become an iconic and influential work known across the world. Its message is empowering: express your message in whatever way you can with whatever you've got.

A meaningful message connects you to people. They tell their friends. Word spreads. Wanting to appeal to a big audience, make a lot of money, impress people, win awards, or whatever distracts us from focusing on what is meaningful.

If you feel like a misunderstood genius, you're not a genius.

A genius knows an idea that isn't communicated is like a car never leaving the factory. It's useless. You want your concept on the road, being driven around, being seen – used. Think of any creative person you admire – they have something to say. But more importantly, they explain their idea in a way you understand.

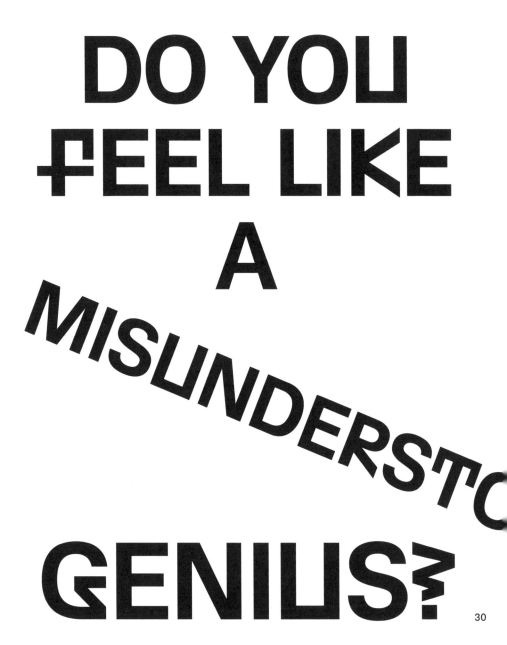

DO YOU FEEL LIKE A MISUNDERSTO GENIUS?

The highly creative are only sometimes natural communicators. But if they've made a significant breakthrough, they know it's essential to find a way to communicate their idea visually.

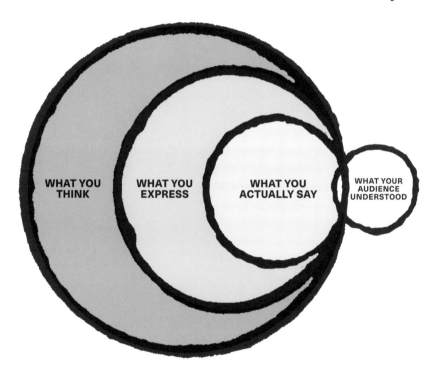

WHAT YOU THINK

WHAT YOU EXPRESS

WHAT YOU ACTUALLY SAY

WHAT YOUR AUDIENCE UNDERSTOOD

We're used to seeing Watson and Crick's diagram of DNA as a spiral – like a staircase. In reality, DNA doesn't look anything like that. It is more complicated and wound tightly together. They created the helix with cardboard cut-outs of individual molecules, moving them around like jigsaw puzzle pieces. It only looks like a spiral when it's unwound – which, in reality, never happens. But the double helix is a simplified image we can all grasp.

If you have a great idea, find a way to make it visual – easy to see means easy to understand.

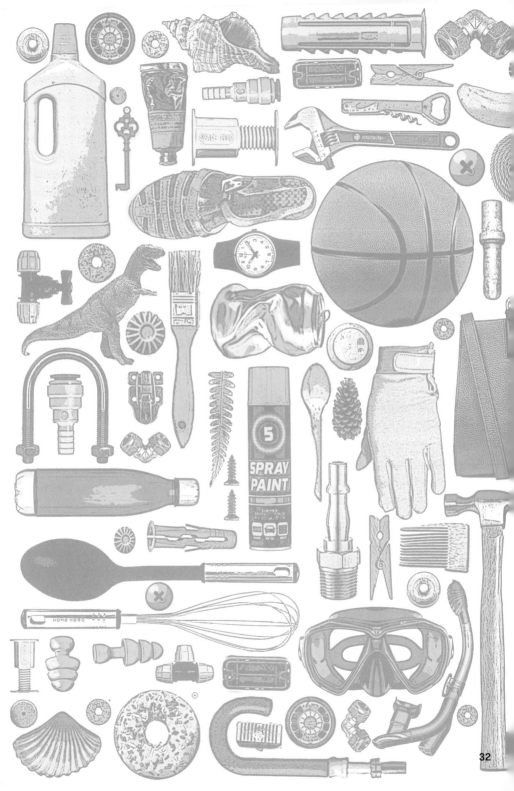

32

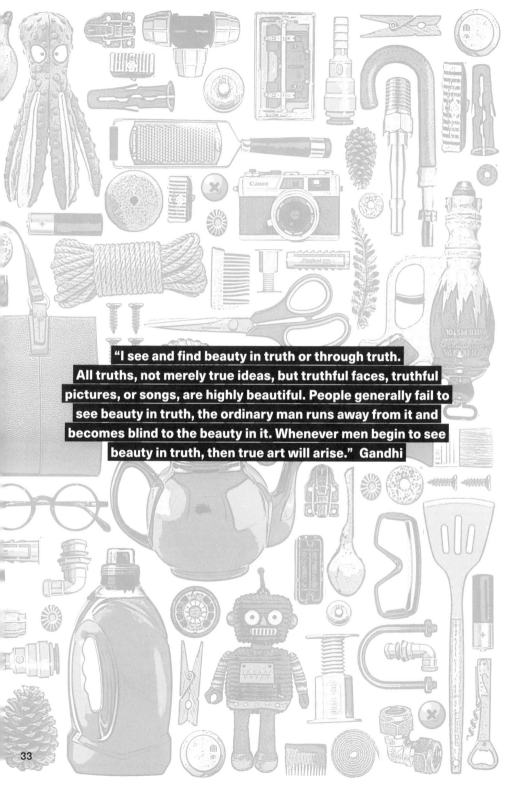

"I see and find beauty in truth or through truth. All truths, not merely true ideas, but truthful faces, truthful pictures, or songs, are highly beautiful. People generally fail to see beauty in truth, the ordinary man runs away from it and becomes blind to the beauty in it. Whenever men begin to see beauty in truth, then true art will arise." Gandhi

How to make your project great

I'm often asked, "How do I make my project great?"
There's a simple answer.

TECHNICAL SKILL

Understand how to use tools

Aware of qualities of materials

Learn and develop skills

Skilful communication of strong concept

Surprising information crafted well

GREAT PROJECT

CREATIVE THINKING

See from multiple perspectives

See old things in new ways

Experiment and accept there'll be failures

Intriguing concept from unusual source

RESEARCH

Investigate the work of others

Search in many different fields

Search with your eyes and hands

I'm sometimes seduced into binge-watching a TV series. It was entertaining, but I wasted several hours. I'm bombarded with the temptation of flippant experiences – flicking through TV channels, websites, and social media.

I admire the artist George Seurat because he shows me that creatives are not passive consumers. They actively instigate a subject they care about.

You spend a lot of time looking through George Seurat's eyes. Seurat set out to develop a great project – to understand how we see. He developed his painting skills, but more importantly, he delved into scientific research on eye optics. He discovered two separate dots of colour close together produced a different colour when seen from a distance. An individual spot of blue and a distinct dot of yellow made green – more intensely than if they'd been mixed together on a palette. Seurat built a painting like a mind, creating an image with dots of pure, unmixed colour. The human mind blended them together. In the 1880s, art critics called his project "Pointillism". "They see poetry in what I have done. No. I apply my methods, and that is all there is to it." said George Seurat.

He discovered the truth of how we see decades before scientists made the same discovery with the help of CAT scans. The eye detects a point of light, a photon, which changes the receptors" molecular structure in the retina. They trigger a chain reaction culminating in a flash of electricity. In milliseconds, the brain transforms the photon into information – dots of colour that form a picture.

Seurat's vision surrounds us. Digital screens and printed pages, are influenced by Seurat's paintings. Dots of pure colour next to each other blend together to make all the intermediate colours. The eye blends individual pixels of colour to create an image. Seurat is an example of an artist changing how others perceive the world.

The first step in any creative project is to look so hard you see how you see. It's not what you see; it's how you see.

Everyone wants to produce something original, but the more you chase it, the more evasive it is. There's a better way.

IT'S BETTER

TO MAKE IT BETTER

"Avant-Garde is French for Bullshit." said John Lennon. I love that he said that. But I was surprised because he was at the cutting edge of music. The Beatles took pop music into new, experimental areas with albums like Sgt. Pepper's Lonely Hearts Club Band. Lennon was married to Yoko Ono, a significant conceptual artist. His bed-in protests outraged and irritated the establishment. So, why the dislike of the avant-garde?

Lennon was annoyed when the art world celebrated something new simply because it was new. "New" means cool. So, we aim to make something fashionable and contemporary. It's better to aim at making things better.

The Beatles work on the Sgt. Pepper album made pop music better. When I listen to it today, it still sounds fresh. They made the lyrics better by ditching the clichéd boy meets girl format. The production broke new ground with unusual sound effects and tape manipulation. The cover was better than any previous ones; it was more conceptual and showed the Beatles posing in front of a tableau of their heroes. It's called the first concept album because there was a theme tying the songs together. They were the first rock band to use diverse influences such as vaudeville, circus, music hall, avant-garde, Indian, and classical music. Critics applauded the album for bridging the cultural divide between popular music and high art. Because of their innovation, albums were seen as a genuine art form. Sgt. Pepper changed pop music for the better. It was an ordinary format, an album of songs. The secret to success is to do an unexceptional thing exceptionally well.

Aim to produce something new and fashionable, and you'll make something shallow and quickly forgotten. Aim to create something better, and you'll make something meaningful.

"We try not to bring out another product that's just different. Different and 'new' is relatively easy. Doing something that's genuinely better is hard." Legendary Apple designer Jonathan Ive

The power of

I always feel uncertain. There are lots of ways I could start this chapter, is this the right one? Is the subject of this chapter interesting enough? Will anyone be interested in this book?

There is more uncertainty in our lives than ever; technology has speeded up change, relationships are more complicated, and we are bombarded with contradictory information by the media. That's a good thing – uncertainty is better than certainty. Uncertainty is the creative person's friend.

of

I've always been fascinated by artist Giacometti because he was so nervous about making art. James Lord wrote an account of posing for a portrait by Giacometti. Each morning, too anxious to start, the painter fussed around the studio for half an hour. Soon after he began, riddled with uncertainty, he stamped his feet and shouted, "I'll die of it".

"not

Giacometti painted over the previous day's work every morning and once said, "...If it doesn't turn out to be any good, I'll give up painting forever." Lord said, 'What consolation was it that the newspapers of many countries spoke of him, that museums everywhere exhibited his works, that people he would never know admired him. None. None at all."

Giacometti was a celebrated artist for decades but began every painting uncertain how to paint. His past achievements were cleared from his mind. But, he said, "Whether it fails or whether it comes off in the end becomes secondary... So long as I've learned something about why."

I love how Giacometti regarded everything as unfinished – even the "finished" paintings hanging in national museums. He was successful precisely because he embraced "not knowing."

Artists and scientists enjoy the state of not knowing more than knowing. They work where there is a why, not where there is a known fact. If you are driven by a why, you can suffer anything. Once a truth is established, artists search for something uncertain.

Only start something when you're sure you don't know what you're doing.

"It seems to me the beginning of wisdom of any kind, including knowledge of ourselves, is acknowledgment of the infirmity of our beliefs and the paucity of our knowledge." Mitchell Green

knowing"

The weakness of knowing

One thing is certain: Richard Feynman, Nobel Prize winner, was one of the most eminent scientists of his time.
The creative way he saw the world was crucial to his ability to solve seemingly impossible problems in quantum mechanics and particle physics.

He summed up his thinking like this…

"You see, I can live with doubt, and uncertainty, and not knowing. I think it's much more interesting to live not knowing, than to have answers that might be wrong. I have approximate answers, and possible beliefs, and different degrees of certainty about different things, but I'm not absolutely sure about anything… But I don't have to have an answer; I don't feel frightened by not knowing things."

It is reassuring that such a great mind was riddled with uncertainty. I don't feel so bad about being unsure. It reminds me if I'm uncertain, I'm in a good, creative place. Bertrand Russell said, "The whole problem with the world is that fools and fanatics are always so certain of themselves, and wiser people so full of doubts."

If you're confident you are right, your attitude is wrong.

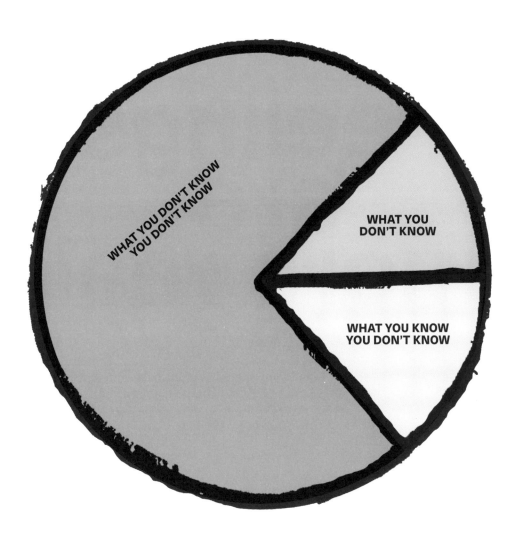

I heard a woman crying. It didn't surprise me. I was in the Mark Rothko room at Tate Modern. There are colossal maroon and black abstract paintings on each wall. People often break down and weep in front of them. I always drop in when passing by because I'm bugged by the question, "How does Rothko produce such a strong reaction?"

Rothko began his career painting objects. If he felt agitated, the brush marks were frantic; if sad, the brush marks were flat and subdued. The brush marks conveyed his feelings. He stopped painting objects and painted how he felt: pure emotion, pure abstraction. He realised feelings were more real than reality.

Feelings are more real

Rothko understood that what you see is not as important as how you feel about what you see. Your personal psychological reality is a powerful truth. You see with your feelings.

In a Rothko painting, I see an echo of my own heartaches and regrets. He makes me feel I am not alone; I'm not the only one who has felt those emotions. It's sad books, films, and paintings that support us when we are miserable, not rom-coms or action thrillers. Someone empathises with us.

What makes your blood boil? What makes you sad? Your message is potent if it expresses your emotions. So, whatever you feel strongly about, don't talk or rant online. Instead, put your feelings into a visual form. Let people see them, and they'll connect more strongly – like the sobbing woman in Tate Modern.

Have you ever had one of those days where you see something that makes your brain start buzzing with questions? For example, how has technology changed the way we see ourselves? Are we more connected in this digital age or drifting further apart? What's the best way to tackle a Tunnock's tea cake? Every day seems to throw up new cultural mysteries that leave me scratching my head.

Work wherever there's a why

Take the Kawaii craze in Japan, for example. It's an obsession with all things cute. I only understood it once I discovered the work of pop artist Takashi Murakami. He questioned why Hello Kitty (a fictional white cat with no mouth) and Pokémon had a massive following in Japan. His paintings and sculptures delve into the attraction of anime and manga. They feature bright, smiling flowers and candy-coloured images of cartoon-like characters with huge eyes and exaggerated bodies. Murakami pulled apart Japanese culture and showed us the tug-of-war between childhood innocence and the adult world.

"In my art I have tried to explain to myself life and its meaning. I have also tried to help others to clarify their lives." Edvard Munch

Anselm Kiefer grew up in Berlin after World War II. Imagine being a child and slowly realizing horrors happened in your own backyard. Kiefer started asking his family about their role in the war. But the recent past was taboo, buried. But he was "so repelled and fascinated" by the Nazis that he wanted to discover how it happened.

"When I was growing up, the Holocaust did not exist. No one spoke about it in the 60s. I felt that there was something hidden... I wanted to know what it was all about." He dived headfirst into exploring it through his art and took a series of photographs of himself wearing his father's Nazi uniform. But Kiefer wasn't trying to stir up drama. In a sensitive, non-judgmental way, he attempted to peel back the layers and unearth what led to such madness.

The artist looks deeply into themselves and their subject. They discover truths. They want to share them with an audience. But they need to attract the audience's attention. So, they present the truths engagingly and surprisingly. To do this, they exaggerate and dramatize the truth. These are lies. But ironically, lies are the most effective way to communicate truths. All communication is a lie because it distorts the truth. But if you distort the truth for the best reason – to make it easier to understand, this gives your life and career purpose and meaning.

The artist doesn't search for answers but to illuminate their subject. Everything is deep – if you dig into it deeply. So, every time you find yourself asking a question, start digging. Trust me, eventually, you'll discover something significant – something that has meaning for you. It will mean so much to you that you'll want to share it. That's when you'll need to lie like an artist.

WHO?

Find a way
to find
yourself

TO BE BELIEVED,

No one will believe what you say
unless they believe in you.
To believe in you, they must trust you.
To be trusted, you must be genuine.

PEOPLE
MUST
BELIEVE
IN YOU

Years ago, I wasn't convinced by Jackson Pollock's drip
paintings. They looked too easy. I thought, "anyone could do
that". Now I'm convinced by those paintings because I believe
in Pollock. He persuaded me he's a great artist. I've seen
hundreds of drawings and paintings he produced during the
twenty years that led to his iconic drip paintings. He made his
process and thinking transparent for all of us to see.

"Trust, honesty, humility, transparency and accountability
are the building blocks of a positive reputation.
Trust is the foundation of any relationship." Mike Paul

Pollock's years of preparation prove Pollock's commitment to the painful exploration of his inner world. He made sacrifices in his personal and professional life for his work. The history of his artistic struggles is laid bare, so I'm convinced. The agitated marks reflect his erratic, hyperactive personality. He died before I was born, but I know him because he was unflinchingly honest and revealed himself in his paintings.

The core of every artist, brand, or organization is believability. I believe Jean-Michel Basquiat, Frida Kahlo, Arnold Schoenberg, and Silvia Plath because they stuck to their core values, whether rain or shine. Their dedication is compelling. I believe what they say in their work because I believe in them as artists.

Words like trust and integrity are old-fashioned in a world of gimmicks and quick fixes. But your most valuable asset is people's belief in you.

TO BE BELIEVABLE BE...

FOCUSED

DEDICATED

MODEST

PERSISTENT

SKILFUL

TRANSPARENT

WHAT YOU DO

How did a waitress, a labourer, and a debt collector get their own retrospectives at the Tate Gallery?

When I ask someone who they are, they answer, nurse, insurance broker, teacher, or whatever. But I wonder, if they lost their job, who would they be then? "Can you remember who you were before the world told you who you should be?" said Charles Bukowski.

IS WHO YOU ARE

"Everyone has been made for some particular work, and the desire for that work has been put in every heart." Rumi

I've always been fascinated by what artists did before they were artists. Julian Schnabel was a taxi driver in New York, Alex Katz was a debt collector in Harlem, Ellen Gallagher was a waitress, and Damien Hirst was a labourer on building sites. But what they did was at odds with who they were. So, they worked at making what they did fit their personalities and ambitions.

"When you make art, people try to stop you from doing it, and everything's sort of designed to stop you from doing it." Said Julian Schnabel. If you spend your time doing things that are not true to you, you must get out of that situation. "It's a great excuse and luxury, having a job and blaming it for your inability to do your own art." Said Schnabel. Schnabel and the other artists dedicated every spare moment to producing work that expressed their true selves.

If I wander around a gallery and stumble upon a Schnabel, it's like meeting a witty and clever friend. It's always uplifting and exciting. What he does is who he is. Bumping into something he did is bumping into him.

I love Schnabel's attitude – no excuses. Go to extraordinary lengths, use every spare second after a day's work when you're tired, early in the morning before work, or when commuting on the train (where I'm writing this). Make sure what you do is who you are.

The private view of my first solo exhibition proved to be a jolting experience. I was used to feedback at art college, which was considerate. But the exhibition audience, drawn from diverse backgrounds, delivered blunt and forthright comments. It was mainly positive, but any feedback can be disconcerting.

Be strong enough

Every painter paints themselves. The chosen subject, style, and medium all unveil your personality. The creative let complete strangers look inside their heads. They expose themselves to close examination that may feel intrusive and uncomfortable.

to

"THE MOMENT THAT YOU FEEL THAT JUST POSSIBLY YOU ARE WALKING DOWN THE STREET NAKED...THAT'S THE MOMENT YOU MAY BE STARTING TO GET IT RIGHT"
NEIL GAIMAN

Artists need a coping mechanism. When I have a book launch or private view, I draw inspiration from Yoko Ono.

A stranger approached Ono with scissors and cut off a piece of her clothing. Ono stayed calm, indifferent. Then, someone else cut off another piece. It was a performance titled "Cut Piece". She sat on a stage and invited the audience, one at a time, to pick up a pair of scissors and cut off her clothing while sitting motionless and silent.

"You change the world by being yourself." Yoko Ono

"Cut Piece" changed the interaction between the artist and the audience forever. It was a metaphor for the role of an artist. Your desk, studio, and gallery are a stage. Not to act and pretend. But to reveal yourself and your ideas. The artist doesn't hide behind a role – not even the role of the artist.

show weakness

To manage the fear associated with vulnerability, Ono employed a Buddhist-like trance. This intentional cultivation of calmness and centeredness becomes a crucial practice for artists, whatever the varied reactions their work might evoke.

Leave a trail

When I begin a workshop, I set a ten-minute drawing project. I've taught long enough to work out each student's character from how they draw – whether confident, methodical, indecisive, or focused. Creativity shows everyone who you are.

It's difficult to understand ourselves. We need to improve our self-awareness because there's a lot we hide from ourselves. That's where creativity is valuable. All art is a self-portrait. Even if you do a painting of someone else. Art helps us find ourselves. It shows us what we care about. "Every good painter paints what he is." said Jackson Pollock.

of

"Every portrait that is painted with feeling is a portrait of the artist, not of the sitter... It is not he who is revealed by the painter; it is rather the painter who, on the coloured canvas, reveals himself." Oscar Wilde

Encountering a creation by Jeff Koons never fails to lift my spirits. Take, for instance, his "Balloon Dog," a piece that speaks volumes about Koons himself rather than merely depicting a balloon dog. In this work, Koons's playful and upbeat personality radiates, celebrating the essence of festivities through an iconic representation of birthdays and parties.

54

The inspiration behind the balloon dog stems from the recognizable shapes twisted from balloons at children's parties. This sculpture is part of Koons's more extensive series, "Celebration," which comprises 20 colossal, impeccably polished stainless-steel sculptures. Among them are a balloon dog, swan, flowers, hearts, cake, and diamonds, all monumental tributes to the symbols associated with joyous occasions. Together, these sculptures evoke the unbridled optimism and wonder reminiscent of childhood.

self-portraits

The mirrored surface of the balloon dog further amplifies Koons's optimism, reflecting his belief that, "Art is something that happens inside us. We look at things in the world, and we become excited by them. We understand our own possibilities of becoming". In essence, Koons's artwork transcends the mere depiction of objects and becomes a medium through which viewers connect with their inner selves.

What you produce tells us who you are. Everything the artist creates is their fingerprint. If you are not leaving self-portraits everywhere, something's gone wrong.

Find someone who's "one of you"

As an art student, I found a deep connection with the obscure painter Anton Räderscheidt. He seemed like a kindred spirit, articulating thoughts I struggled to express. His work resonated with me and illuminated a path I could follow.

We all aspire to create something uniquely our own, but our artistic journey often begins by emulating those we admire most. This initial path can lead to a garden teeming with possibilities or become a confining prison cell if we get trapped in another artist's style. It's disheartening when people view your work, and instead of expressing admiration, they remark, "I love Edvard Munch too," casting you as a mere impersonator.

Tracey Emin avoided this pitfall. She acknowledged her connection to Munch, stating, "I think mainly I just felt emotionally that "he's one of me," "I'm one of him," and that he was my friend in art". Emin embraced Munch's approach of personal disclosure, turning her art into a half visual diary and half personal revelation, even if it meant exposing painful truths. For Emin, the essence of beauty lay in honesty, no matter how difficult it might be to confront.

Emin didn't mimic Munch's style; instead, she absorbed his attitude. Her work bore a distinctiveness rooted in her own life experiences and disclosures. Munch was a guiding influence, but Emin's artistic journey took its own course, resulting in a unique expression. Established artists like Emin find solace and inspiration in kindred spirits, leaning on their support throughout their careers.

The lesson here is clear: an artist you admire should act as a springboard for your creativity, not an armchair to linger in. While they may show you the way, your ultimate destination is yours.

Don't listen to life-lies

People often tell me that because I've written five books, I must have tremendous confidence in my writing. My answer is, "No, just the opposite". When I wrote my first book, I was naïve and didn't know how hard it was. I just wrote it and sent it off. When I set out to write this book, my head was filled with doubting voices telling me a publisher wouldn't be interested, it wouldn't appeal to readers, and many other reasons. I reminded myself of psychiatrist Alfred Adler, who discovered we tell ourselves "life-lies".

We convince ourselves a problem is too difficult to overcome and don't even try. We believe we'll fail because of our history, the people in power, the political system, or whatever – so there's no point. Not trying is easier than trying. Adler uncovered two ways we deal with difficulties.

Adler discovered a positive attitude led to having a go and a sense of fulfillment – even if you failed. A negative approach led to feelings of guilt that we could have achieved something great if we'd tried.

"The more scared we are of a work or calling, the more sure we can be that we have to do it." Steven Pressfield

Adler's research proved it was better to try because even if you fail, you feel good about yourself. "Courage," Adler said, "is not an ability one either possesses or lacks". The courage to overcome doubting voices in our heads is not something we're born with; it has to be developed.

We can learn to enjoy challenges. Or we can see obstacles as insurmountable and not even try. I still propose books to publishers and get rejections. Hopefully, this book will end up in a bookshop and in your hands. If it doesn't, I'm satisfied that at least I tried.

DON'T BELIEVE EVERYTHING YOU TELL YOURSELF

"To be successful you must be unique, you must be so different that if people want what you have, they must come to you to get it." Walt Disney

When traveling in London, I'm so intent on getting from A to B; I'm like a zombie. I'm blind to the amazing things around me. On the tube and the streets, I'm surrounded by other zombies who've shut their eyes to what's happening around them.

"In the land of the blind, the one-eyed man is king" is a proverb. It means someone who has never been considered unique can shine – if they have an insight that others have missed. That's the role of an artist.

How to open your eyes

I love the work of Eduardo Paolozzi. He showed me how the city was a machine. We are moved by escalators, pavements, lifts, and tube trains. We become part of the mechanism – we become robotic. Living in London, I remind myself of this every day when I realise I'm behaving like a thoughtless cog; I fight against it. I also love Nam Jun Paik because he showed me the importance of embracing technology and being conscious of its effects on me for good and evil. I'm deeply indebted to Barbara Kruger. She revealed to me how the media influence my perception. I'm conscious of her ideas whenever I read a magazine, watch TV, or use social media. These artists had a unique insight. They showed me things I was blind to.

If we're not in a state of constant awareness, we're missing opportunities. Whenever I get confused, I remind myself my role is to uncover the overlooked and share the discovery.

You can't be too sensitive

Do you often find yourself grappling with guilt over your heightened sensitivity? Do you experience emotions more intensely than others, leading to accusations of being "too sensitive" or an "overthinker"? If so, you may identify as a "highly sensitive person" or HSP, a term coined by psychologists. While society tends to focus on the challenges HSPs face, there are substantial benefits to harnessing these traits for creativity.

WHAT PEOPLE THINK A HIGHLY SENSITIVE PERSON IS LIKE

Too irrational and emotional

WHAT A HIGHLY SENSITIVE PERSON IS ACTUALLY LIKE

Empathetic

Deep Thinkers

Intuitive

Creative

Acutely Aware

Intensely perceptive

Far-sighted

Extremely observant

62

According to the Nobel Prize-winning novelist Pearl S. Buck, the truly creative mind is characterized by abnormal sensitivity. For HSPs, "…a touch is a blow, a sound is a noise, a misfortune is a tragedy, a joy is an ecstasy, a friend is a lover, a lover is a god, and failure is death".

Research by psychologists has demonstrated that sensitivity is a valuable asset for creativity in several ways. HSPs, due to their heightened awareness, possess a deeper understanding of their thoughts and emotions, facilitating more articulate expression. They excel at noticing subtle details, giving them a unique perspective on everyday life.

HSPs also exhibit intuitive decision-making abilities, bypassing the need for constant analysis. Their natural and effortless approach to learning distinguishes them, making learning creative skills enjoyable rather than a chore. Moreover, their ability to blend diverse ideas and concepts effortlessly contributes to their creative dexterity.

Observant of others' feelings and able to empathize easily, HSPs excel in understanding their audience, a valuable trait for writers, filmmakers, and marketers. As a minority in the population, highly sensitive individuals perceive society through the lens of outsiders, offering a unique perspective that enhances the originality of their work.

Given their heightened receptivity to stimuli, HSPs have a wealth of information to draw upon in their creative endeavours. Their unique problem-solving processes, which see opportunities in challenges and unconventional solutions, set them apart from the majority, making them a valuable asset in creative fields.

If you are made to feel bad about being highly sensitive, remind yourself it's insensitive people who are the problem.

I often feel overwhelmed by the abundance of easy options, whether takeaways, ready meals, or the constant rush of fast-paced living. But what truly bothers me are the rigid structures of political ideologies, commonly called "Isms".

Keep to this formula — avoid formulas

"You are the books you read, the films you watch, the music you listen to, the people you spend time with, the conversations you engage in. Choose wisely what you feed your mind." Jac Vanec

Political Isms close doors, limiting our perspectives and constraining our thinking. In contrast, Art Isms serve as a gateway to expanding the mind. For instance, Impressionism highlights the ever-changing nature of light and the world. Cubism reveals that our perception is not confined to a single viewpoint but encompasses multiple angles simultaneously. Surrealism delves into our subconscious desires, bringing them to the forefront of our awareness. When Picasso sensed that Cubism had become a formula, he promptly abandoned it. Similarly, Giacometti, an originator of Surrealism, moved on when it became predictable. Artists recognize formulas as traps to avoid. The idea of declaring oneself a Cubist today seems absurd, as it's over a century old. Conversely, many political ideologies have been around for even longer, yet people follow these old formulas religiously.

Political Isms are akin to fast food for the mind. On the contrary, art movements nourish thought processes. Art Isms encourage independent thinking, urging individuals to form their own opinions. In contrast, political Isms dictate how we should think, resulting in a loss of individuality.

Our minds, like our bodies, consume what is available. To foster creativity, we need fresh, mind-expanding ideas. Staying true to personal vision enhances individuality and improves society as a whole.

I've experienced being fired, and although it felt like a disaster, it ultimately became a blessing. The same was valid for filmmaker Tim Burton. Back in the 1980s, Disney was struggling with bland and unsuccessful films. Seeking fresh ideas, they brought in Burton for his original vision. However, Disney's corporate structure was uneasy with his unconventional ideas, leading to his dismissal. Producer Don Hahn mentioned Burton was let go for being "too quirky".

If you've never been fired, you've got an attitude problem

Despite being fired, Burton's quirky films found success, prompting Disney to rehire him. Yet, after creating the eccentric film "Frankenweenie", he was fired again for its perceived eccentricity.

Undeterred, Burton intensified his distinctive style. Disney eventually hired him a third time and successfully re-released "Frankenweenie". Burton's journey proves that what may seem unconventional to some can be ground-breaking to others, and he became one of the most respected film directors.

Similarly, when I lost my university position, I was initially horrified, especially with the responsibility of supporting two young children. However, this setback pushed me to seek a position in other universities. I found one that aligned better with my values and collaborated with people who understood me. Had I not been fired, I would still be stuck in the wrong job in the wrong place. In the creative industries, experiencing multiple firings is often seen as a positive indicator of entrepreneurial spirit.

"Getting fired is the best thing that could happen to any of us. That way, we'd quit treading water and do something with our lives." Chuck Palahniuk, Fight Club

Find the right audience for your message

You don't know what you've created

I'm immersed in my creative world when I write or paint in solitude. I explore personal interests and put those ideas onto paper. But the true essence of any creation only emerges when I share it with an audience. The act of unveiling art is transformative; it evolves into something unforeseen and sparks a dialogue with the external world, challenging the artist's initial perspective. I had a concept for this book, but its true meaning will only be revealed through the reactions of others.

until someone sees it

A work of art is a tangible manifestation of an artist's innermost thoughts. The artist may not crave attention, but their creation yearns to be seen. A work of art longs for an existence beyond the artist's studio. Art seeks public attention not out of egoism or a desire for recognition but as an inherent part of its nature. The work comes to life only when it resonates with others.

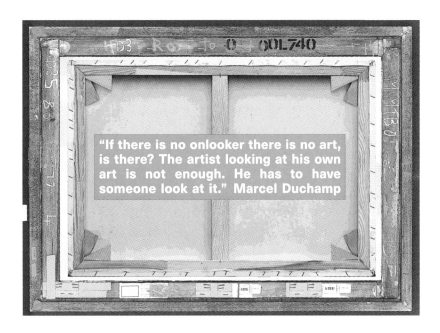

"If there is no onlooker there is no art, is there? The artist looking at his own art is not enough. He has to have someone look at it." Marcel Duchamp

I can't tell you how many times I wrote something thinking it expressed one idea, only to find people saw something else in it. When an artist presents their work, a metamorphosis occurs within the work and the artist. The audience's reactions actively reshape the artist's understanding. Ultimately, the work's meaning is determined not by the artist but by the audience... Picasso once showed a mixed-media drawing of a guitar to the collector Roland Penrose. Penrose thought it was a woman. Picasso's attitude was that if you see a woman, it's a woman. The audience has a pivotal role in refashioning the art.

Finding an audience is synonymous with finding yourself. When the artist discovers their audience, they, in turn, discover new dimensions of their own identity.

This throws the idea of creating solely for personal satisfaction out the window. Filmmaker Martin Scorsese encapsulates this sentiment, "When I'm making a film, I'm the audience". He steps outside himself and tries to see with the eyes of the audience.

Artistic creation transcends individuality when exposed to the gaze of others. The reader of this book (you) will have a transformative effect. Art is a bridge between the personal and the collective. This exchange is the essence of artistic self-discovery.

Ever talked to a wall? That's what it feels like whenever I've had to get the approval of a committee or board for a project. It's a nightmare when you've got an important idea to share but an audience that won't listen. Florence Nightingale found a solution.

HOW TO TALK TO A BRICK WALL

$\left(\begin{array}{c}\text{and} \\ \text{make it} \\ \text{understand} \\ \text{you}\end{array}\right)$

She had an important message to communicate to a brick wall. She discovered that the biggest killer of soldiers in the Crimean War was not the injuries from battle. Instead, poor hygiene in hospitals caused disease that killed three out of every four soldiers. Improved hygiene would save tens of thousands of soldiers' lives.

She explained the problem and her solution to the generals and military authorities (the brick wall) in a meeting using statistics, facts, and information. They listened attentively. When she left, they instantly forgot and carried on as before.

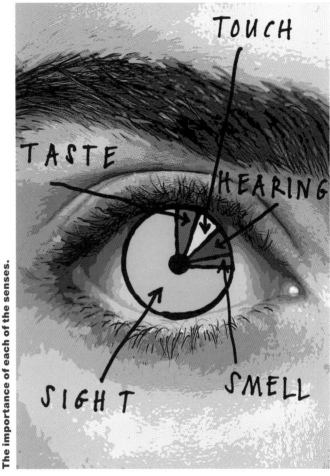

The importance of each of the senses.

But then Nightingale did something astonishing. Days later, she returned with the world's first-ever pie chart. She visualised the statistics. Once the generals saw Nightingale's pie chart, her message was unseeable. So, they put her reforms into action. As a result, the survival rate of soldiers rose by 75%. Army hospitals, and every hospital, was improved forever.

We're visual animals.
Picture your idea or be ignored.

I guard my mind like a fortress. I'm cautious about the ideas I allow to infiltrate my thoughts. In a world bombarded with the incessant clamour of "Click here!" or "Two for the price of one!" I staunchly defend against the pollution of my mental space. Opening the floodgates to every fleeting pop-up ad would turn my brain into a chaotic trash can.

HEAD FOR THE HEART

But here's the conundrum: how can an artist breach the defences and implant their idea into my mind, or anyone else's, for that matter? Clever, brilliant, and incisive ideas are admirable but insufficient against the formidable barriers we construct.

Every time I see Edward Hopper's painting "Nighthawks", it strikes a profound chord within me. I've lived that scene. I relocated from a quaint country village to the bustling heart of London and found myself a stranger in a strange city. Hopper's painting shows four anonymous people in a New York diner at night.

They are sitting close, yet psychologically, they're miles apart. Their gazes never meet. Hopper captured a universal truth: the loneliness experienced amid a teeming metropolis. His art becomes a conduit for his idea, revealing that the very structures of modern life – buildings, cities, technology – distance us from each other. Hopper doesn't merely convey dry facts; he makes us feel them.

"Art-making is not about telling the truth but making the truth felt."   Christian Boltanski

In communication, directing your message solely to the intellect is futile. Your message must touch a person's heart to open their mind. Hopper's art becomes a key that unlocks the door to my mind, not through logical argument but by evoking an instinctive response.

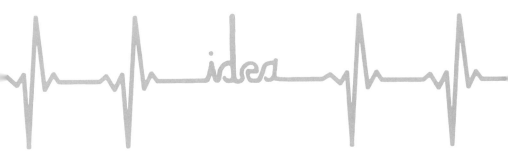

The key to effective communication is targeting the heart rather than the head. In the grand symphony of ideas, the harmonious chord struck in the heart echoes the loudest, reaching over the barriers of scepticism and intellectual fortresses. If "The eyes are the window of the soul", the heart is the door to the soul.

Transport them from their THERE, to your HERE

We want to show others how we see the world. But it's difficult because they see the world from their perspective, which might be very different from yours. It's easy to have a point of view and shout it out. But it takes creativity to persuade others to see things your way. So, transport them into your world, and they have no choice but to be submerged in your vision.

When artists create a painting, poem, or advertisement, they construct an alternate reality. Each artwork functions as its own universe, drawing the viewer in. An exhibition amplifies this immersive experience, presenting a cohesive world. For instance, a solo exhibition at the Guggenheim is a Basquiatworld or Monetland, compelling us to

FOUR

be totally surrounded by their vision. Similarly, shops, websites, cinemas, and concert halls offer distinct environments. Just as Disneyworld reflects Walt Disney's imagination, walking down a street exposes us to diverse visions: Pradaland, KFCland, M&M World, Legoland, etc. Even urban planning shapes our surroundings, creating distinct landscapes. Watching a film like Pulp Fiction transports us to Tarantinoland.

Many artists feel alienated within societal norms, prompting them to carve out their own space – an alternative reality. This personal realm is a sanctuary for creative expression, allowing free rein to abstract ideas and intuition.

You're a world-builder. A painting, sculpture, advert, story or song is a piece of the jigsaw that creates your world. Inviting audiences to step inside our creations encourages them to lend us their imagination. Consequently, reflecting on our motives is crucial: Why are you constructing this world? What insights are you delivering? What new perspectives do they gain? When they step out of your world and back to reality, what are they taking with them? Ultimately, it's about leaving a lasting impression and enriching others' understanding.

When creating work, I often wonder: should artists speak to enduring posterity or immediate popularity? Marcel Duchamp had a surprising and enlightening answer.

HOW TO HAVE

As a teenager growing up in 1970s England, it was cool to be into underground, cult, and independent bands. The cultural vibe demanded music with socially aware lyrics, progressive themes, and a rebellious punk attitude. In stark contrast, ABBA's unabashedly commercial pop music was deemed uncool by serious music critics who ridiculed them.

As time passed, those who felt like social outsiders found solace in ABBA's music. Their songs became prominent features in films like "Muriel's Wedding" and LGBTQ+ films like "The Adventures of Priscilla, Queen of the Desert", resonating with audiences who didn't conform to mainstream norms. ABBA's appeal grew as people appreciated their catchy tunes infused with genuine emotion and pristine studio production.

"Why should I care about posterity? What's posterity ever done for me?" Groucho Marx

Duchamp, a provocateur, challenged conventional beliefs by asserting that the audience's judgment held greater significance than the artist's. In his view, the artist produced nothing until the onlooker had declared, "You have produced something marvelous". He considered the public as the ultimate arbiter of artistic merit.

From Shakespeare to The Beatles, the artists whose goal was instant impact, ironically achieved a lasting legacy. Their desire for immediate popularity paved the way for enduring masterpieces. Duchamp believed the audience, not the artist, has the final say on a work's significance.

Decades later, ABBA's legacy endures through stage shows like "Mamma Mia!" and films, maintaining their relevance while many of the once-cool indie bands have faded into obscurity, their names and songs forgotten.

Duchamp's philosophy encourages artists to root themselves in the present, recognizing that predicting long-term posterity is impossible. He emphasizes the importance of the public, stating, "I give to the onlooker more importance than the artist, almost, because not only does he look, but he also gives a judgment". This underscores the profound influence of public perception. The audience becomes the final judge, holding the power to have the last word.

The artist doesn't have to concern themselves "It is just as vulgar to work for the sake of posterity as to work for the sake of money." Orson Welles with posterity because, ultimately, the audience will decide. Our only option is to do the best we can here and now. If your work touches on a profound truth, people will still relate to it in a hundred years.

THE LAST WORD

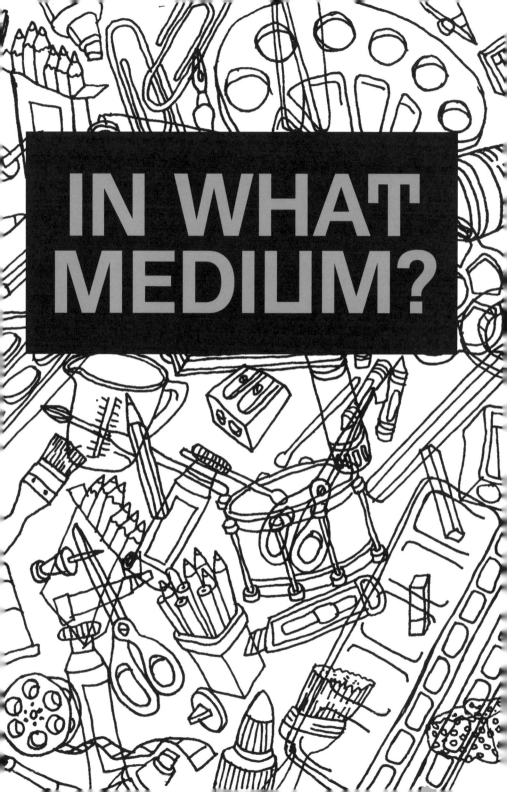

IN WHAT MEDIUM?

Find the best
medium to give
your message
impact

Ever made a pick axe from deer antlers, arrows from flint, or fishing nets from a vine? Neither have I, but making anything with your hands is satisfying. I'm writing this with pen and paper before it's transferred to a computer. The feel of the nib against the sheet adds to the experience.

The way to find your way

But we live in a technological, screen-based world. We've lost touch with touch. Stone Age people always handled natural objects, which helped them find the best way to use them. The material spoke to them, and they listened. They had a conversation.

"When we are no longer children, we are already dead." Brancusi

82

Our DNA has mostly stayed the same in the last one hundred thousand years. Mould a piece of clay, and you're doing what you evolved to do. Your brain and body are working in harmony – nothing is more rewarding.

When Constantin Brancusi was a child, he was famous in his Romanian village for carving simplified wooden farm tools. He continued as he grew up but made sculptures of figures and animals. He simplified them to the point they were seen as ultra-modernist and futuristic. He was driven to capture "not the outer form" but "the essence of things." He let the feel of the material guide him, whether the grain of the wood, the texture of limestone, or the crystals in marble.

"Every master knows that the material teaches the artist." Ilya Ehrenberg

When he was a wealthy, internationally successful artist, Brancusi continued to dress in simple Romanian peasant clothes. In his home, there was a big slab of rock as a table and a primitive fireplace; he made his own furniture out of wood. When wealthy collectors, royalty, and dignitaries visited, Brancusi cooked them traditional Romanian dishes.

"Truth to materials" is a term that describes how every medium has unique qualities. The more sensitive we are to those qualities, the better the work. If you need help, let materials guide you.

KISS is an invaluable method used in design to remind ourselves to –Keep It Simple, Stupid!

KEEP!

Keep to your message. We begin with a direct, powerful idea. But as a project progresses, we let it become complex. Keeping to one core idea requires intelligence.

How to

IT!

"It" is your core message. Precisely, what do you want to say? Is "it" worthwhile? Artists sometimes worry that a direct message is one-dimensional, but an idea can be both succinct and profound.

Rachel Whiteread – made the invisible visible. Volvo cars – keep you safe. Sartre – we are responsible for ourselves. Dali – our unconscious mind is our true self. Duracell batteries – long-lasting. Cindy Sherman – identity is a construction of media stereotypes. They all had one core message.

SIMPLE!

Even experienced artists fall into the trap of overcomplicating their message. "Make everything as simple as possible, but not simpler." said Albert Einstein. For people to remember your message, it must be simple. However, simple doesn't mean bland, unintelligent, or stupid.

KISS

"Three Rules of Work: Out of clutter find simplicity. From discord find harmony. In the middle of difficulty lies opportunity." Albert Einstein

STUPID!

Even the most intelligent artists make the stupid mistake of being too elaborate. "Genius is making complex ideas simple, not making simple ideas complex." Albert Einstein. It takes intellectual rigor to keep things simple.

Going from

unknown

When you're small, humble, and unknown, how do you get attention in a field dominated by the big, loud, and famous? If you're an unknown artist, a tech start-up, a new restaurant, or whatever – you're providing something worthwhile – so you need people to notice.

In 1950s America, Doyle, Dane, Bernbach titled their new start-up advertising agency DDB after their names. They joked they should have called it "Two Jews and an Irishman" because all the big advertising agencies were run by white Anglo-Saxon protestants.

They faced a problem we all face when starting a new venture – how to grow. The US had mega companies, big burgers, massive skyscrapers, and huge cars. American advertising agencies were gigantic, with huge receptions, plush offices, and big budgets.

DDB was small. Their office was tiny and out of the way. They were outsiders, anti-establishment underdogs – an advertising agency that was anti-advertising. Bill Bernbach thought differently than other advertising executives. He thought like an artist. He wanted to communicate the truth about the products he advertised.

DDB won the Volkswagen car account. American cars, Cadillacs, Pontiacs, and Chevrolets were huge with massive chrome grilles and flamboyant tail fins. Car ads showed beautiful girls in mink coats swooning over rich men. But the VW Beetle was small, slow, foreign, and ugly. World War II was a recent memory, and Volkswagen's association with Germany made it unpopular. Nevertheless, Bernbach and Volkswagen were kindred spirits – small maverick foreigners trying to create an impact in a land dominated by the gigantic.

"Getting your product known isn't the answer. Getting it WANTED is the answer." Bill Bernbach

Bernback promoted the truth. He came up with the "small is beautiful" campaign. They explained how being small was an attribute. They persuaded the public that buying a Volkswagen Beetle meant you were an audacious, clever maverick. It worked. The Beetle sold millions. DDB won the award of "greatest advertising agency ever" by the industry.

to

Bernback applied the thinking of artists to advertising – discovering the truth about something and highlighting it. Advertising had become an art. The most potent component of advertising is the truth.

When you're small, you have little to lose. There's no pressure. You can take huge risks, like running radical and original ad campaigns. You can make edgy and ground-breaking films, exhibitions, or books. You don't have to consider your reputation, colossal studio, staff, or agents. If you're unknown, make the most of your freedom.

known

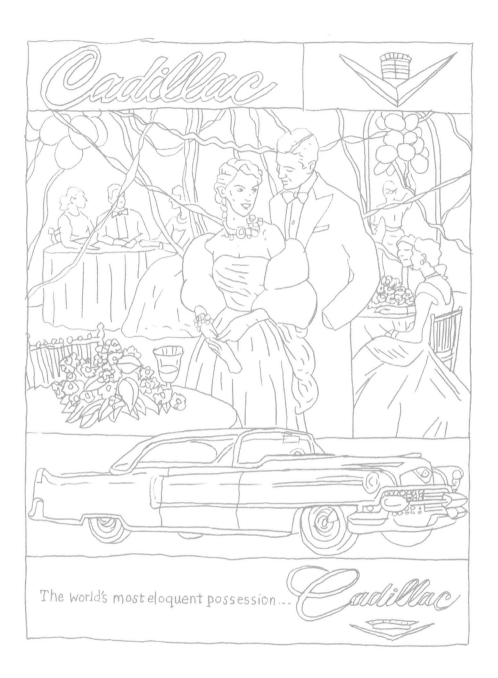

A rough sketch of a Cadillac ad circa 1960.

Think small.

A rough sketch of the iconic Volkswagen ad circa 1960. It makes the Cadillac ad look ridiculously pompous and overblown.

If words fail,

Sometimes, words are not adequate to express what I want to say. Fortunately, the philosopher Ludwig Wittgenstein provided me (and you) with a solution.

In 1914, Wittgenstein read an account of a courtroom trial about a car crash. Each of the many witnesses described the incident. The judge needed clarification. He asked for a miniature model of the street with cars and human figures so that each witness could show him the accident using the model. Now he could see the incident, he understood.

here's the route

It made Wittgenstein realise the purpose of words was to create a picture in our minds. We describe something. The other person sees the image. Communication goes wrong because the picture people create in their minds differs from what we intended. Our words weren't accurate enough.

The witness's words didn't create the right picture in the judge's head. They described reality inaccurately. The judge needed a model so he could see what happened.

to success

Much of our unhappiness is caused by our inability to describe our thoughts and feelings to others. Wittgenstein believed language was a bottle and we were a fly trapped inside. Therefore, we must escape from the bottle (language). The way out is to visualise what we think and feel (like the model).

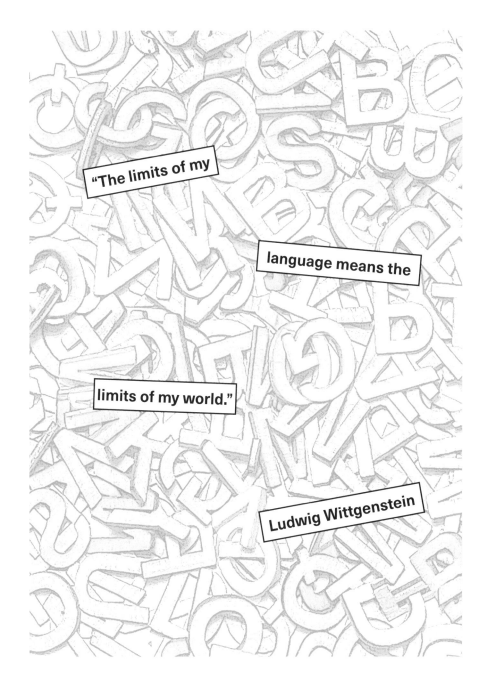

"The limits of my

language means the

limits of my world."

Ludwig Wittgenstein

All his life, Wittgenstein surrounded himself with artists and
musicians. He was fascinated by their ability to create a
personal language – a way to express subtle thoughts and
feelings. If you want people to get your message, you must
show them, not tell them.

How to make

If you have an essential idea, you want it to stick in people's minds. Ideas are like eels; they're often hard to grasp and slip away – even if the concept is clever and vital. An idea is useless if it isn't fixed in the audience's memory. Artists use six principles called STICKY to create unforgettable images.

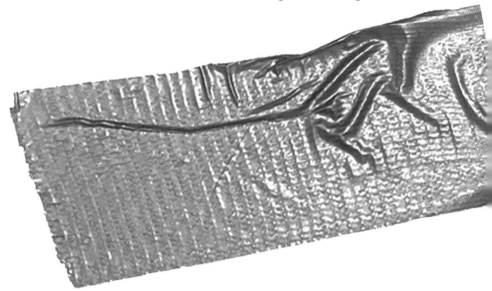

Dali knew how to make an idea memorable. Once seen, a Dali soft watch is unseeable. It's an idea about time. It reveals how we perceive time. A watch is a factually accurate, scientific measure of time. But Dali reveals the more profound truth about time. Time feels malleable. An hour seems like five when we're waiting on a platform for a train. But an hour seems like five minutes when we're at a party. A soft watch expresses this idea in an unforgettable image. Once seen, it's an image you can't unsee.

Dali was a master of the rules of sticky ideas. Surprise: a melting watch is shocking and gets the audience's attention. Trust: Dali's watches are convincingly realistic. Your message must show your idea is concrete and believable. Important: Establish the core, most important point of your message, and don't deviate from it. Clear: Dali leaves you in no doubt what you are looking at. Kiss: Dali dipped into our subconscious emotions. Your idea must stir feelings to make people care. Yarn: Dali explained the story behind each of his paintings. Convey your message in a narrative.

Anyone with a good idea and these principles can make an idea sick.

youʀ idea
sticky

Put the right

Walking down a street in London, I was shocked to see a Monet in a gold frame hanging on a wall. An information plaque was placed next to the painting – like in a gallery. Artist Banksy had secretly hung some of his street art in major public galleries, so the National Gallery in London responded by putting their works out in the streets. They hung over 40 works on walls in London. I stood there and watched; almost every passer-by stopped and looked. If it had been a poster, no one would have noticed. A poster would have been the right thing in the right place.

"If you have a statue in the city centre you could go past it every day on your way to school and never even notice it, right. But as soon as someone puts a traffic cone on its head, you've made your own sculpture." Banksy

You expect paintings in a gallery and graffiti on outside walls. However brilliant they are, they are in the right place, so they go unnoticed. We fall into the trap of putting things where they are supposed to be. Put the right message in the wrong place, and it stands out. An ad for a Harley-Davidson motorbike? Put it in a mother and baby magazine instead of a motorbike enthusiasts' magazine. If you produce creative work, you have to be creative about where it's placed.

Want your work to stand out? Where is the most surprising place it could be placed?

94

message in

the wrong place

STOP

When I wrote this chapter, I was pleased with its clarity. But my editor misinterpreted it. I looked at it again and realised two or three poorly chosen words distracted them from the message.

being

It happens to even the best artists. Francis Bacon was painting a picture titled "Crucifixion". He'd nearly finished but thought a figure lacked something, so he added an armband with a small, barely visible, smudged swastika. It was a design decision. Unintentionally, the swastika dominated the painting. It's such a powerful symbol the viewer's eye went straight to it. Everyone assumed the picture was about the Nazis. The painting had nothing to do with the Nazis. The swastika was noise, a distraction. Bacon deeply regretted it and said, "…it was stupid to put in the swastika, but there it is. I didn't think about it, I didn't think that people would interpret it all the different ways they have".

erstood

In art and design, "Noise" is anything that distracts the audience from your message. Every detail is essential. You might think your message is unmistakable, but a small element, a misplaced symbol, or a misspelled word will cause your audience to get the wrong message. Attention to detail isn't about perfection. It's about striving for the highest quality.

Wherever there is noise, silence it.

Attention to detail✓

misund

It's easy to let social media seduce you into projecting a more exciting life than you're actually living. The people who post the truth about their work and lives are the most impressive, like Ai Weiwei.

It's challenging to be as open and honest about yourself as Ai Weiwei is. Unfortunately, the Chinese government decided Weiwei was subversive and put fifteen surveillance cameras around his house/studio to monitor who came and went.

"Technology is a liberation. I think the information age probably is the best thing to happen to the human race in human evolution. Now you have the equal opportunity to equip yourself through information and knowledge and express yourself as an independent mind." Ai Weiwei

Weiwei responded by putting his own cameras inside his home and studio; one was even positioned over his computer. They broadcast live 24 hours a day on his website. He showed everyone what he was doing all the time. It was a way of declaring he had nothing to hide. As a result, he got millions of views. Ai Weiwei embraced transparency.

"Content is fire. Social media is gasoline." Jay Baer

The Chinese government applied old thinking to a new medium. Ai Weiwei used new thinking in a new medium. "In my life, there is so much surveillance and monitoring... my phone, my computer... Our office has been searched, I have been searched, every day I am being followed, there are surveillance cameras in front of my house", he said. Weiwei didn't use social media to impress people. He used it to simply show them whatever he was doing. The more honest content you share online, the more people relate to you. Digital platforms suit artists because they know how to show truths on a visual medium.

"It's a dialogue, not a monologue, and some people don't understand that. Social media is more like a telephone than a television." Amy Jo Martin

therefore I AM

The fantastic thing about modern media is its ability to reveal truths using images. We need to help it, not hinder it.

WITH WHAT EFFECT?

Have the effect you intended

State the truth, and some people will be outraged. The truth can be complicated. Sometimes, it requires us to rethink what we believe. It challenges our beliefs or perspectives. But an artist can't change the truth to make it palatable.

DON'T KISS WITH A LIE SLAP WITH

The public was shocked by the image. It showed a ship sailing across a violent sea. The crew jettisoned the cargo – African slaves. A blood-red sunset turned the waves copper. A leg belonging to a naked woman jutted out of the stormy water, an iron chain fastened to her ankle. Other bodies thrashed in the waves.

The painting, The Slave Ship, by William Turner, captured an actual event. The slave ship didn't have enough drinking water for 132 slaves. If slaves died of thirst, owners received no insurance. So, the captain ordered them to be thrown overboard so insurance could be collected. The case went to court, but no one was found guilty because no law had been broken. The public was mainly indifferent. Then, Turner's painting of the event was exhibited in London at The Royal Academy of Arts in 1840.

The exhibition was filled with flattering portraits of London's elite or nude women languishing in lush interiors. Turner's painting stuck out like a sore thumb. It caused outrage. Writer Mark Twain declared, "The most of the picture is a manifest impossibility – that is to say, a lie…" Nevertheless, the lie conveyed the truth better than all the previous anti-slavery campaigns and speeches.

Turner's paintings were too radical for much of the public, and he was used to being an unpopular outsider. It's tempting to tell people what they want to hear and be liked, but Turner showed we must put the truth out there, whatever the consequences. It's better to be slapped with the truth than kissed with a lie.

"The poet, the artist, the sleuth – whoever sharpens our perception tends to be antisocial: rarely 'well-adjusted', he cannot go along with currents and trends. A strange bond exists between antisocial types in their power to see environments as they really are." Marshall McLuhan

THE TRUTH

Your style should be instantly identifiable from a glimpse.
These are my rough sketches after Jackson Pollock and
Coca-Cola. Their identities are immediately recognisable.

"An artist must be the kind of person that can change the world by way of transforming him or herself." Zhou Zan

Sometimes, I find myself saying something and then questioning whether it truly represents my own thoughts or if it's just a trendy idea I've picked up from the media. It's hard to think independently when there is so much pressure to conform. That's why I believe that being true to yourself is the most revolutionary thing you can do. It's not always easy though, and that's why we need support. Personally, I find inspiration from other artists who encourage me to be myself. If they can be true to themselves, then so can I.

During my time in New York in the 1980s, I was introduced to the work of Keith Haring, and it shocked me. Haring was courageous enough to create art about issues that mattered to him, such as gay rights and HIV/AIDS, which were considered taboo at the time.

Keith Haring's iconic messages were plastered all over the walls of New York City. Then galleries noticed his work and exhibitions followed. As the HIV/AIDS epidemic began to spread, fear and stigma also spread, especially towards the gay community. Despite this, Haring persevered in his art and activism, using his work to raise awareness about AIDS and raise funds for life-saving drugs.

Though artists may not set out to change the world, their creativity has the power to amplify even the smallest of voices. By being true to themselves and their art, they have the ability to reshape our perceptions of the world, ultimately leading to positive change.

The minimalist sculptures created by artist Donald Judd have had a significant impact on modern kitchen design. The Wachowski sisters' film, The Matrix, showcased how digital technology can alter our perception of reality. Boccioni's sculptures influenced the streamlined design of vehicles such as cars and motorcycles. These artists did not intend to revolutionize our ideas, kitchens, or means of transportation, but by staying true to their unique artistic vision, they managed to change the world for all of us.

"Art changes people, people change the world." John Butler

The word "brand" makes me shudder because of its links to commercialism and selling out. But the truth is that because great brands deeply understand their identity and communicate it effectively, they're successful.

HELP!

In the 1960s, most artists wanted to be like Willem De Kooning, Jackson Pollock, or Mark Rothko. They were appreciated by a cultural elite but unknown to the general public. Andy Warhol horrified the art world by declaring he wanted to be like Coca-Cola (to the abstract expressionists, it was an example of everything wrong with America). He didn't want to be an elite artist producing elite works for the elite. Instead, Warhol wanted to reach ordinary, everyday people. Like Coca-Cola, he tried to create mass-produced, cheap work accessible to everyone.

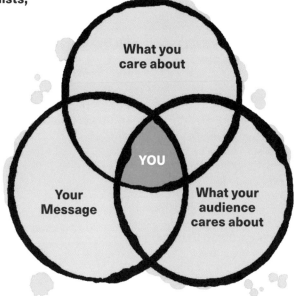

What you care about

YOU

Your Message

What your audience cares about

Warhol knew the comparison with Coke would offend everyone in the art world, but he saw a truth: the artist is a brand. They laughed at him, but this original thinking was the key to his success. Warhol liked Coke because "A Coke is a Coke, and no amount of money can get you a better Coke…" The President, Liz Taylor, or a homeless person drank the same Coke. That's why Warhol didn't describe his workplace with the prestigious term "studio". Instead, he called it "The Factory".

A brand is a business with a distinct identity, style, design, ethos, and advertising that distinguish it from competitors. Because Warhol thought of himself as a brand, he clearly understood what he was trying to achieve. This made him refreshingly truthful about marketing himself. He was candid about finance: "Making money is art, and working is art, and good business is the best art." Truthful about employing assistants: "This way, I don't have to work on my objects at all. One of my assistants or anyone else, for that matter, can reproduce the design as well as I could." Honest about his profession: "Art is anything you can get away with".

Ironically, Pollock, Rothko, and de Kooning became the thing they hated – brands. They were businesses (their work sold for millions) with a distinct identity created with an ethos, style, and design that distinguished them from competitors. Look in the gift shop when they have a major retrospective.

If you think of yourself as a brand, you realise what drives you and how to get that across to an audience.

Who am I?

Enter through the gift shop

It's natural to aim for the top of your profession. But is the top where you think it is? When I visit prestigious galleries, the grandiose, quasi-religious atmosphere of the white cubes intimidates me. Everyone speaks softly, and no one eats, drinks, or laughs. On the other hand, I feel at ease in the gift shop, where everyone feels free to talk, and laugh.

The art world elite sneers at the reproductions on postcards, tea towels, biscuit tins, pencil cases, and mugs. They believe they trivialize serious art. But when I relate to an artist, a reproduction on a tea towel, postcard, or whatever helps me remember them and what they are about.

When I use the tea towel, it keeps the artist's work alive in my mind. The artist's spirit is with me when I clean crumbs from the toaster or wash up. The ideas in the reproduction rub off onto us and support us when we're worried about our children, jobs, or the chaos of modern life. It's a signpost pointing the way. Our connection with the reproduced image is honest and genuine.

Rather than imagining your work in the main gallery of the Guggenheim, consider it on a tea towel in the gift shop. It may seem humble, but it's honest and authentic.

You probably don't think about it or intend it, but when you create art, you create reality. Artists make work, which creates a sense of who we are as a society. Your art creates our culture. Oscar Wilde said, "Life imitates art far more than art imitates life."

Your art creates reality

Life sometimes imitates art in obvious ways.

In the 2015 film Spectre, James Bond chased a villain through a Day of the Dead Parade in Mexico City. The scriptwriters invented the parade to make the chase exciting. Truthfully, the Day of the Dead was a private, family affair. But tourists who had seen the film were disappointed when they visited Mexico, and there was no parade. So, the authorities created one – including the props from the movie. Now, it's an annual event. The film created reality.

Life sometimes imitates art in subtle ways.

In Hollywood films, individualism was celebrated – a hero stood up to injustice and corrupt authority and triumphed. Women had jobs, cars, and independence and were treated as equals. This contrasted with the culture in many countries that put group harmony and submission to authority above individual expression. Hollywood introduced them to ideas about individuality and self-determination. Hollywood movies promoted ideas about freedom for the individual without intending to.

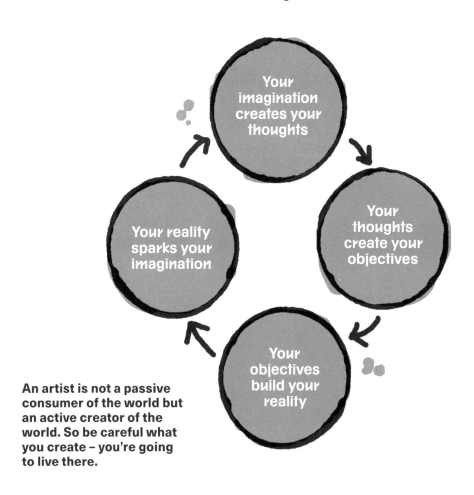

Your imagination creates your thoughts

Your thoughts create your objectives

Your objectives build your reality

Your reality sparks your imagination

An artist is not a passive consumer of the world but an active creator of the world. So be careful what you create – you're going to live there.

As an art student, visiting an exhibition by artist Max Ernst changed my life. He revealed a way of looking at the world that freed up my thinking and has stayed with me forever.

It's logical to be

WARNING
THE 3RD FLOOR
HAS BEEN
TEMPORARILY
MOVED TO
THE 7TH FLOOR

When I travelled through London to see a Max Ernst retrospective, I focussed on getting from A to B. I saw what I needed to see. I crossed the road when the "green man" lit up, jostled with commuters in suits on the tube, and read the complimentary newspaper.

In the Max Ernst exhibition was a sculpture titled "Gift." A flat iron with nails glued to its surface. It was unusable, absurd. But in doing so, Man Ray made me aware of how ridiculous it was before. A heavy lump of iron had to be heated on a stove and then used to flatten clothes. Why flatten clothes with a block of metal? We accept normal behaviour without question. Man Ray highlighted that what we have been taught to believe is logical is ridiculous.

"The fact that an opinion has been widely held is no evidence whatever that it is not utterly absurd." Bertrand Russell

On the way to the exhibition, I saw absurd things but didn't notice how ridiculous they were. On the way back, wherever I looked, I saw absurdity. The exhibition changed my perception. A sign declared, "Insane gas prices ahead." Someone had used a mattress as a temporary gate. A car was upside down by the side of the road. Strangers crammed against each other in the tube, like sardines, pressing their faces against someone's armpit. Absurdity was everywhere.

ABSURD

Man Ray gave me a sense of freedom, not only in my work but also in my life. He informed me that logical behaviour like wearing a suit and commuting was ridiculous. When I realised standard conventions were absurd, I wasn't afraid to do what others thought was ridiculous – like become an artist. In a world that didn't make sense, I could seek my meaning wherever I liked.

Do you

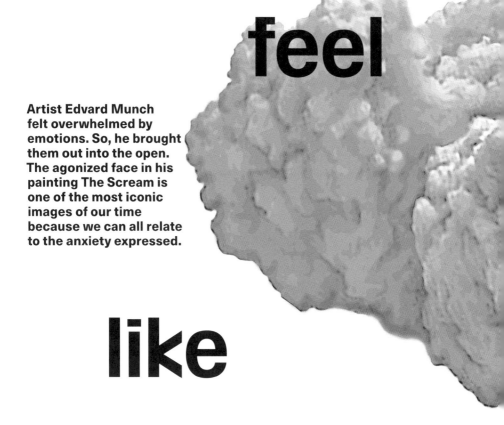

Ever felt like screaming? I live in London and often feel like screaming at the chaos, traffic, expense, rudeness, and overcrowding. Looking around, I see people take it out on others by being insulting or lashing out. It's healthier to let it out and scream – onto paper.

feel

Artist Edvard Munch felt overwhelmed by emotions. So, he brought them out into the open. The agonized face in his painting The Scream is one of the most iconic images of our time because we can all relate to the anxiety expressed.

like

"I think there is a contradiction in an art of total despair, because the very fact that the art is made seems to contradict despair." David Hockney

Art is a way to confront our demons. When you're brave enough to reveal your struggles with them, others relate to those anxieties. In turn, they feel more confident to reveal their demons. Munch's honesty in revealing his angst inspired many artists and led to the expressionist movement.

We all have toxic thoughts running around in our minds, causing havoc. Art is a net to catch those demons and dissect them. If I feel like screaming (which is often), I draw the scream on paper. That way, the emotions are external to me, and easier to examine. Give it a try. Whatever you feel angry, happy, or infuriated about, put it into visual form – a poster, a social media post, a painting – and suddenly, you've taken control of them.

screaming?

Working in the arts, I often get lost in a tangle of concepts, theories, and fashionable ideas. We become distanced from everyday life. But there's a way to get down to earth.

Each shop in the street had a sign outside describing their services, such as grocery, light shop, baker, tailor, and doctor. One sign read, "The True Artist Helps the World by Revealing Mystic Truths." It hung in the window of a shop the artist Bruce Nauman had converted into a studio. Nauman looked at the other stores and thought he should have a sign, too. The others sold essentials, bread, light bulbs, vegetables, or whatever. Nauman was a conceptual artist who also produced and sold things like the other traders.

Nauman said, "It was a kind of test – like when you say something out loud to see if you believe it. Once written down, I could see that the statement […] was on the one hand a totally silly idea and yet, on the other hand, I believed it. It's true and not true at the same time."

I admire the honesty of Nauman's sign: admitting he was selling – just like everyone else. Creative people are often embarrassed about commerce. But asking questions like, "Who's financing this?" or "Who's making money from this?" is a reality check.

I SELL THEREFORE I AM

What would your shop sign say?

Politicians, religious leaders, and authorities often assert themselves as trustworthy experts with all the answers. That's why I don't trust them. I only trust someone who is honest enough to admit that they may not have the answers.

The artist Rene Magritte was walking down the road. He noticed the baker had the word "baker"on a sign over their shop. The butcher had a sign with the word "butcher". The cobbler, "cobbler", and so on. But the tobacconist's sign had no words, just an image of a pipe. Magritte realised we read images the same way we read words.

He went straight home and painted "La Traihson des Images" ("The Treachery of Images"). It is a painting of a pipe. Underneath the pipe are the words "This is not a pipe."

Magritte lied when he wrote, "This is not a pipe" because we can see a pipe. But the painting is an illusion of a pipe. The title, "Treachery of Images", tells you the truth, that the picture is an illusion. Magritte is saying, "Watch out, I'm manipulating you". He's also reminding us that all images are illusions, and they are all manipulating us.

120

Tell everyone

It's easy to get lost in the pleasure
of making illusions (lies) and forget
the purpose you're making them
(revealing the truth).

you are lying

Don't trust anything I've written here, I'm manipulating you.

Be

dead

serious

Whenever I'm near Highgate Cemetery I can't resist dropping in to see the shocked reaction of passers-by's to the gravestone of artist Patrick Caulfield. There's laughter, horror and curiosity. Now and then, someone will slowly get Caulfield's message. I watch the realisation spread across their face. These are the reactions an artist hopes they'll trigger.

Caulfield's gravestone is a huge matt piece of granite with the word "dead" cut-out of it. There's no name, inscription – nothing. The gravestone is like his work – straight to the point. His gravestone reflects the thinking behind his paintings. His art described things in the barest way. outlined in black. Caulfield was simultaneously dead serious and dead funny.

The reason I love his gravestone is because it stands out from all the others due to its blunt honesty. It sits among statues of weeping women and kindly angels. The design and wording of most tombstones are clichés and with inscriptions like "dancing with the angels" or "forever in our hearts'. I love that Caulfield designed the gravestone himself and thought deeply about it. He knew it would contrast with the rest of the graveyard.

I go there because it reminds me that too often, I fall in line with what is expected of me when I should be questioning the status quo and being true to myself.

about jokes

Some truths about the truth...

"The truth is more important than the facts." Frank Lloyd Wright

"Art does not exist only to entertain – but also to challenge one to think, to provoke, even to disturb, in a constant search for the truth." Barbara Streisand

"Truth is like fire; to tell the truth means to glow and burn." Gustav Klimt

"Art is a microscope which the artist fixes on the secrets of his soul, and shows to people these secrets which are common to all." Leo Tolstoy

"Humour is something that thrives between man's aspirations and his limitations. There is more logic in humour than in anything else. Because, you see, humour is truth." Victor Borge

"We taste and feel and see the truth. We do not reason ourselves into it." William Butler Yeats

"The two words 'information' and 'communication' are often used interchangeably, but they signify quite different things. Information is giving out; communication is getting through." Sydney J. Harris

"If we all worked on the assumption that what is accepted as true is really true, there would be little hope of advance." Orville Wright

"There are two distinct languages. There is the verbal, which separates people... and there is the visual that is understood by everybody." Yaacov Agam

"How can one learn the truth by thinking? As one learns to see a face better if one draws it." Ludwig Wittgenstein

"I cross out words so you will see them more; the fact that they are obscured makes you want to read them." Jean-Michel Basquiat

"I shut my eyes in order to see." Paul Gauguin

"The truth of art lies in its power to break the monopoly of established reality to define what is real." Herbert Marcuse

"A feminist is any woman who tells the truth about her life." Virginia Woolf

"The story-maker... makes a Secondary World which your mind can enter. Inside it, what he relates is 'true': it accords with the laws of that world. You therefore believe it, while you are, as it were, inside. The moment disbelief arises, the spell is broken; the magic, or rather art, has failed." JRR Tolkien

"Nothing is truer than truth. All the mistakes committed by great artists are due to their having separated themselves from truth, believing that their imagination is stronger." Joaquin Sorolla

"The difference between the artist and other people is that the artist is more inclined to say the truth." Yaroslaw Rozputnyak

"Since there is no such thing as absolute rightness and truth, we always pursue the artificial, leading, human truth. We judge and make a truth that excludes other truths. Art plays a formative part in this manufacture of truth." Gerhard Richter

"Minimalism is the pursuit of the essence of things, not the appearance." Claudio Silvestrin

"Art is not a mirror held up to reality but a hammer with which to shape it." Bertolt Brecht

Acknowledgements...

Thanks to Louis Judkins for his invaluable advice on the text and images throughout the development of this book. Special mention to Zelda Malan for her advice on the imagery and layouts. Thanks also to Scarlet Judkins for her astute points and help in all areas of the books development.

Thanks to Studio Bergini for transforming the book with their great layouts and design.

References...

Magee H. 9 Easy Ways You Can Speak Your Truth Today. Tinybuddha.

Petridis A. (2019). Madonna: "I wanted to be somebody – because I felt like a nobody." The Guardian newspaper.

Clayton V. (2015). The Needless Complexity of Academic Writing. The Atlantic.

Osho, (1998). The Book of Secrets, Three Looking Techniques. St. Martin's Griffin.

Punj R. (2017). Joana Vasconcelos Explains Contemporary Kitsch. The Culture Trip.

Willett B. (2014). 12 Things Highly Uninspired People Do. Lifehack.

Gandi M. (1919). Young India.

Dave. (2010). Seurat & The Psychology of Geometry: Point by Point. Madampickwick.

De Botton A. (2004). The pleasures of sadness. Edward Hopper. TATE ETC.

Popova M. The Artist's Reality: Mark Rothko's Little-Known Writings on Art, Artists, and What the Notion of Plasticity Reveals about Storytelling. The Marginalian.

Rothko M. (2006). The Artist's Reality – Philosophies of Art. Yale University Press.

Emin T. Interview with Devaney for exhibition catalogue.

Lee J., Ogawa H., Kwon Y. and Kim K-S. (2018), Spatial Footprints of Human Perceptual Experience in Geo-Social Media. MDPI.

Hockley W. (2008). The picture superiority effect in associative recognition. PubMed.

Tomkins C. (1964). Interview with Duchamp. New Yorker Magazine.

Sanouillet M. and Peterson S. (1975). The Essential Writings of Marcel Duchamp. Thames and Hudson.

Bates R. (2014). Erasing Duchamp. The Paris Review.

Interview with Bruce Nauman. (1980). Archives of American Art, Smithsonian Institution.

Smith K. (2012). Jenny Holzer. Interview Magazine.

Lai A. (2012). Chinese artist Ai Weiwei places himself under home surveillance. CNN.

Twain M. (1880). A Tramp Abroad. American Publishing Company.

Pendle G. (2014). Patrick Caulfield's Epitaph? Dead, Of Course. Frieze.

Strickler Y. (2023). Worldbuilding is creative resilience. The Ideaspace.

The image in the chapter *I Link Therefore I Am* is inspired by a Banksy work, *What are you looking at*. Take a look at his book, *Wall and Piece*. Century. 2005, it's been a huge inspiration to me writing this book.

The paint dribbles on the page about branding is my sketch after Jackson Pollock, as is the sketch of the Coke logo.

The image of the tombstone carved with "the end" is my drawing after *The End 1516 Toilet Paper Limited Edition Stool* by Maurizio Cattelan and Pierpaolo Ferrari.

The painting in *Put the Right Message in the Wrong Place* is my version after Monet.

I recommend...

Steal Like an Artist by Austin Kleon. I've been recommending this book to my students for years. It's essential for any creative person.

Think Like an Artist by Will Gompertz is a book I return to again and again. Check it out.

Ignore Everybody: And 39 Other Keys to Creativity by Hugh MacLeod is full of invaluable advice.

Made to Stick: Why Some Ideas Take Hold and Others Come Unstuck by Chip Heath and Dan Heath is the best book on communicating ideas that I've read.

Other books by Rod Judkins

Make Brilliant Work
Make Brilliant Work is for individuals seeking success but feel limited by their talent, skills, or knowledge. In Make Brilliant Work, you will learn from cutting-edge research in art and design, psychology, and science. The book explores a range of case studies to show how creative success is not the result of talent or intuition but practical, step-by-step processes.

Ideas Are Your Only Currency
Turn your mind into an idea factory. This interactive book will prepare you for a fluid, global, and interdisciplinary world by helping you become an innovator and "ideas person". The 100 interactive exercises will develop your ability to think up great ideas quickly and easily and solve problems.

The Art of Creative Thinking
Have you ever been in a situation where you needed a creative solution but lacked the methods or processes to solve the problem? In 87 chapters, The Art of Creative Thinking provides 87 secret techniques successful creative people use to innovate and invent.

Contemporary Collage with Figurative Painting
Collage is an innovative and exciting technique invigorating the artistic process through unusual associations and dislocated imagery. This practical book explains the fundamental techniques and shows how collage can be used to portray the figure in new and challenging ways. It is written for both novices and experienced artists.

Change Your Mind:
57 Ways to Unlock Your Creative Self
Your mind is not fixed; you can transform yourself no matter your age or previous experience. Change Your Mind will show you how creativity is a skill you can benefit from, whether working towards an exhibition, trying to start your own business, composing music, or being more innovative in the office.

About the author

Rod Judkins is a writer, artist, creative innovation consultant, and university lecturer. He has written six books, including *The Art of Creative Thinking* and *Change Your Mind: 57 Ways to Unlock Your Creative Self*, which have been bestsellers and translated into over fifteen languages. Judkins has delivered workshops and talks on creative thinking to numerous businesses worldwide, including Apple, Google, Samsung, The Royal Free Hospital London, Bombay Sapphire, and many others. He has lectured on art, design, and creative process at Central St Martin's College of Art for many years. His international reputation as an alternative thinker has seen him lecturing on platforms as diverse as Tate Modern, University College London, The London School of Economics, ESCP Europe, the University of Navarra, The University of Lisbon, and the University of Namur.

COLOPHON

BIS Publishers
Borneostraat 80-A
1094 CP Amsterdam
The Netherlands
T +31 (0)20 515 02 30
bis@bispublishers.com
www.bispublishers.com

ISBN 978-90-636-9707-5